REAL ESTATE CROWDFUNDING

The differences between Equity and Lending Crowdfunding

Antonio Costanzo

1

Table of Contents

WHAT IS REAL ESTATE CROWDFUNDING

Crowdfunding is the collection of money from a large group of individuals in order to finance a project, start-up company, or campaign and is usually done through the internet. This method of pooling together small amounts of money for an expensive goal appears to be spreading to investments that require a large amount of capital - specifically, real estate.

Crowdfunding is a new tool for raising money for businesses and an easier way to access such ventures for investors. It utilizes social media outlets like Facebook, Twitter and LinkedIn to reach an audience of potential investors. The idea behind crowdfunding is that many people are willing to invest a small amount, and when they do, large sums of money can be raised quite quickly. It opens doors for businesses to investors they could never reach otherwise.

In the past, real estate development was only available for investment through private equity in the development company or through real estate investment trusts (REITs) and was not feasible as a direct investment for most individuals. This is because each real estate development venture is a finite project, and registering each product as a security, even under Regulation D filings, is inefficient. Furthermore, real estate developers were not allowed to actively market or solicit investments for their projects due to restrictions by the Securities and Exchange Commission (SEC).

As the concept of crowdfunding was growing, the Jumpstart Our Business Startups Act of 2012 modified certain rules under Regulation D that opened the door for more direct marketing and solicitation to accredited investors. Now, real estate developers can rely on crowdfunding sites to solicit investments from high-net-worth investors who are eager to make an investment in this market. The SEC is reviewing material in an attempt to open this market up to all investors, but for now, crowdfunding sites must classify each investor to ensure they qualify to make private investments in real estate in this manner. It is the hope that the online investment market for real estate will flourish in the coming years, giving investors a great alternative.

Currently, real estate crowdfunding has become popular in the United States, partially due to new legislation that permits the raising of funds online; however, different laws in Asia may hinder the growth of these new investment platforms.

In Singapore, for example, the Monetary Authority of Singapore (MAS) regulates the collection of public funds, but not the real estate market. Because of this, a way to use crowdfunding has been to purchase international property (in this case, property not located in Singapore), through a fund collection platform based in Singapore.

One Singaporean website is doing exactly this. CoAssets.com collected over SG$3,000,000 from over 1,300 users during their first six months of operation. Individuals are able to invest in real estate developments located in Malaysia, Thailand, Philippines, Australia and China.

While crowdfunding is still in its infancy, there are several different reasons why it could become the next big thing in the Asian property market. If one really thinks about it, co-ownership of properties has already been done for decades worldwide. The only difference is that by using the internet as a distribution channel, the process is made less bureaucratic and expensive by eliminating fees, numerous middlemen and complexity. Crowdfunding is merely an evolution of what already is.

Smaller developers will benefit from crowdfunding's rise as well. Banks are generally hesitant to loan property developers amounts between SG$1 million and SG$10 million because of their fees not being worth the additional paperwork. SMEs would be given an alternative to bank financing.

Crowdfunding will also make the property market more accessible for investors by giving them an ability to purchase part of an apartment, office building or retail store: types of property that typically have higher rental yields than a residential unit, but are prohibitively expensive to most individuals.

But while real estate crowdfunding seems like it will eventually make its way across the Pacific from the U.S., the risks, lack of regulation, anonymity by both parties and other issues make some skeptical. While crowdfunding is inarguably a success for some types of transactions, as websites such as Kickstarter and IndieGogo prove, time will tell whether investors in Asia can benefit from it.

REAL ESTATE CROWDFUNDING VS OTHER INVESTING OPTIONS: A COMPARISON

Let us take a quick step back and let you know we are not telling you that real estate investing should be where you park of all of your investment capital. This section has been written to compare real estate investing via crowdfunding to what we consider the other main investment vehicles out there. This way if you have been considering investing in real estate you have a place for a quick comparison.

Let's look at some year-to-date real estate trends across the country according to Realtor.com.

Median Sales Price Days on Market Active Listings

Median Sales Price

- $280K (up 8%)
- United States
- $521K (up 4%)
- Boston, MA
- $196K (up 8%)
- St. Louis, MO
- $949K (up 6%)
- San Francisco, CA

In general, you can see that the country's real estate market is up as a whole. Additionally, the days on market and active listings are declining which means the real estate market is strong.

What does this mean for real estate investors? The short answer is that it is a great time to invest some of your money in real estate. Using crowdfunding as a vehicle to invest in real estate, you can start with as little as $500 and should expect 5-8% annualized returns at a minimum without any startup or investing fees. Additionally, some of the crowdfunding platforms are offering profit sharing.

Stocks

Let's dig into the stocks. Surely, many of you are already thinking of investing in the stock market. One of the most striking things we found when looking into investing in the stock market is that many stock market firms have fairly high minimums. Additionally, all brokerage firms have trading fees that range from $10-30 per trade. That can put a serious dent into your investment capital. Both of these are in direct contrast to investing in real estate via crowdfunding where the minimum is $500 and you will not pay any fees to invest your money.

Mutual Funds

Another common investment strategy is mutual funds. Investing in mutual funds does allow you to invest smaller amounts of money, as little as $50-100/month, but there are still fees. Most funds have a management expense ratio (MER) charge each year and sales charges when mutual funds are purchased. Again, with real estate these types of fees do not exist.

Savings Accounts

Lastly, we wanted to include the run of the mill savings account as an investment strategy. Average savings account rates range from 0.32% to 1.55% annually according to mybanktracker. Need we say more about this option?

To summarize, there are definitely options for you to invest your money. We think based on the low minimums and lack of investing fees that investing in real estate via crowdfunding should be an option in your portfolio.

REAL ESTATE CROWDFUNDING PROGRESS

Before the internet, real estate syndication required that interested investors have an established network of syndicate partners to find trustworthy, profitable deals to buy shares of.

Like the two guys opening up a bar together, the guy with the bar experience had to somehow meet the guy with the money, and vice versa. Fast forward a few years and things have really changed for real estate syndications, with the help of the internet and the advent of crowdfunding.

Real estate crowdfunding gives access to the financial fundamentals of a deal and makes it easy for accredited investors to purchase shares without using the old model of country-club small talk and caddy fees.

Crowdfunding is a way to raise money through the internet for a big project with the help of a 'crowd' of investors; if a project gets enough funding, it's a "go", and if not, the money is returned to investors.

Crowdfunded real estate syndications are more accessible, have lower investment minimums and offer a wealth of online project information available to potential investors.

HOW REAL ESTATE CROWDFUNDING WORKS

Real estate crowdfunding lets you invest small amounts of money, sometimes as low as $500, in either the equity or debt of a real estate project or portfolio. In return, you own a proportional stake in either the property/portfolio or its underlying mortgage and receive payments in the form of quarterly or monthly dividends.

When you invest via a real estate crowdfunding platform, you become a limited partner in the investment- which can vary by project. You really need to look at the project when deciding. Some projects are debt-based, meaning that you are providing a loan that is secured by the property. Some projects are debt-based, but you're actually investing in a third-party note tied to the performance of the underlying real estate investment.

Some projects are equity-based, which means you are investing in a fund, such as a REIT, which holds a property or multiple properties and you'll receive cash flow as well as some of the upside in appreciation.

Many companies only require a $5,000 minimum investment in a project, so the barrier to entry is relatively low. The companies also charge fees of up to 3%, which may be a shock for those used to investing in low-cost mutual funds and ETFs. You may not see these fees directly, since they are typically paid out of the return prior to paying you.

Real estate crowdfunding is an effective way for investors to pool their financial and intellectual resources to invest in properties and projects much bigger than they could afford or manage on their own.

The basics of real estate crowdfunding aren't all that different from two guys opening a bar together. As the manager and operator of the deal, the Sponsor invests the sweat equity, including scouting out the property, raising funds and acquiring and managing the investment property's day-to-day operations, while the investors provide most of the financial equity.

The Sponsor is usually responsible for investing anywhere from 5-20% of the total required equity capital, while investors put in between 80-95% of the total. Obviously, the more the Sponsor can invest in the property, the better for investors since investors want to see as much "skin in the game" as possible.

Syndications are simple to set up and come with built-in protections for all parties. They're usually structured as a Limited Liability Company or a Limited Partnership with the Sponsor participating as the General Partner or Manager and the investors participating as limited partners or passive members. These LLCs are also sometimes called Special Purpose Vehicles where the real estate crowdfunding platform and the investors in the platform have NO claim on these SPVs or LLCs.

The rights of the Sponsor and Investors, including rights to distributions, voting rights, and the Sponsor's rights to fees for managing the investment, are set forth in the LLC Operating Agreement or LP Partnership Agreement.

REAL ESTATE CROWDFUNDING PROFITS

Profits are made through rental income and property appreciation and sale.

Rental income from a syndicated property is distributed to investors from the Sponsor on a monthly or quarterly basis according to preset terms. A property's value usually appreciates over time, so investors can net higher rents and earn larger profits when the property is sold.

Payment depends upon the time the investment needs to mature; some types of syndications are over within 6-12 months while others can take 7-10 years. Everyone who invests receives some share of the profits.

The Sponsor will propose a Target Date for exit, but such target dates are just rough estimates. If the target date so happens to be in the middle of a bear market, it may be prudent to keep holding on and collecting rent until the cycle turns.

At the deal's beginning, the Sponsor may earn an average acquisition fee of 1% (although it can be anywhere from .5 to 2% depending upon the transaction). Before a Sponsor shares in the profits for their work as manager and promoter, all investors receive what is called a 'preferred return.' The preferred return is a benchmark payment distributed to all investors that is usually about 5-10% annually of the initial money invested.

An Example Of A Real Estate Crowdfunding Investment

Real estate crowdfunding investments are structured so that the sponsor is motivated to ensure the investment performs well for everyone. Let's look at an example of a preferred return.

If you're a passive investor who invests $100,000 in a deal with a 10% preferred return, you could take home $10,000 each year once the property earns enough money to make payouts possible.

After each investor receives a preferred return, the remaining money is distributed between the Sponsor and the investors based on the syndication's profit split structure.

If, for example, the profit split structure is 70/30 — investors net 70% of the profits after receiving their preferred returns and the sponsor nets 30% after the preferred return.

For example, after everyone receives their preferred return in a 70/30 deal, and there is 1 million remaining, the investors would receive 700k and the Sponsor would receive 300k.

Real Estate Crowdfunding Statistics

- In 2012, over 47,000 investors participated in syndications.
- The average size of a real estate offering was 2.3 million.
- Passive investors came up with 80-95% of the initial capital investment
- Sponsors came up with 5-20% of the initial capital investment
- Investors received a preferred return ranging from 5-10%.
- The average preferred return was 8%.
- Sponsors netted an acquisition fee of .5 to 2%. The average acquisition fee was 1%.
- Sponsors netted a property management fee between 2 and 9%.

TYPES OF REAL ESTATE CROWDFUNDING INVESTMENTS

The two common types of real estate crowdfunding investments are equity investments and debt investments. With equity investments, you're either investing in the project or a portfolio of projects while with debt investments you're investing in a mortgage or group of mortgages. Equity investments are usually longer term investments that offer higher returns and are more common.

The 2 types of real estate crowdfunding investments include:

1. Crowdfunding Equity Investments

Equity investments offer investors a passive, indirect ownership position, which means they're a long term investor and receive a return on their investment from property appreciation and rental income. The investor is a shareholder in a specific property or a portfolio of properties, and in return for their investment, they receive a proportionate number of shares.

Equity investments generally earn returns through:

- Rental income
- Asset price appreciation

Since the projects are usually either new developments or need extensive renovations, the investments are for longer time periods, generally 3 – 10 years. Investors are generally paid through quarterly cash flow distributions where the investor receives a return on their investment through a proportional share of the rental income the property generates. Since the properties are professionally managed, you don't have to do anything but invest your money and sit back.

The other (although less common) way equity investors receive a return on their money is through asset price appreciation when the property is sold. These equity investors will also get certain tax advantages – such as depreciation deductions – that real estate debt crowdfunding investors don't receive.

There are two types of equity investments. The first is common equity investments while the second is preferred equity investments. Some crowdfunding sites only offer one type of investment. Still, we will show the benefits and drawbacks of both in the table below and discuss each component in detail.

COMMON EQUITY VS. PREFERRED EQUITY CROWDFUNDING INVESTMENTS

Common equity is where you buy into the actual project being developed and receive a percentage ownership of that project. Platforms give investors proportional rental profits, either monthly or quarterly. What's more, if the project appreciates in value, you receive a portion of it once the property is sold.

However, it's considered the riskiest type of real estate crowdfunding investment. This is because common equity investors are repaid last, and if the property doesn't appreciate as planned or doesn't generate enough cash flow, you can lose your investment. However, the potential for a high ROI is the greatest, since common equity investing doesn't have a cap on its return like preferred equity does.

Preferred Equity Crowdfunding Investments

Preferred equity is kind of in between common equity and debt crowdfunding in terms of risk and the order of repayment. It's not as risky as common equity but not as safe as loans. Preferred equity investments generally pay out fixed returns based on rental income. Like debt investors, preferred equity investors usually receive monthly payments, but similar to common equity, they can take advantage of tax deductions.

However, returns are typically fixed for preferred equity investments, giving them less of an upside than with common equity investments. Still, they're paid back before common equity investors and therefore isn't as risky.

Regardless of the specific type, the pros and cons of equity investing include:

Pros:

Higher returns on your investment when compared to debt investing.

Since most equity deals are set up as an LLC, so you receive depreciation deductions similar to if you owned an investment property.

Lower fees than investing in debt; annual fees are usually 1 – 2%.

Cons:

Higher risks since equity investors are second in line to be paid back after loan investors.

The risk of the property not performing and not getting your money back since you're investing in the equity, not the debt, so you can't receive proceeds through a foreclosure.

Your money is held up for a longer time period, so limited liquidity, most hold times range from 3 – 10 years

2. Crowdfunding Debt Investments

Crowdfunding projects are usually funded with one or more loans, and these loans can be partially funded from your investment. In return, you receive income in the form of an interest rate spread. Essentially, your funds are being borrowed by the real estate developer with the intention of paying you back plus interest once the loan matures.

The loan that you invest in is secured by the property being built. The typical investment term is 6 months – 2 years and the average return is 8.5 – 9.1%. As with all crowdfunding investments, you don't choose when to exit the investment and get your money back. The exact timeline will be set in a signed agreement up front.

Debt investments are generally categorized as syndicated debt or platform issued debt. Some crowdfunding sites only offer one type of debt, but we will show the basics of both in the table below including a detailed breakdown of each.

SYNDICATED DEBT VS PLATFORM ISSUED DEBT CROWDFUNDING INVESTMENTS

Investors who invest in debt syndication are investing in a portion of an existing real estate loan that was originated by professional lenders (considered the middlemen). These middlemen provide extra security on the loan since they diligently research it before approving it, but they also add to the fees. Debt syndication fees average 0.5% – 1.5% annually.

Investors receive fixed payments that usually offer 8% – 12 % returns. The debt is secured by the property, so it's less risky than an equity investment. Terms are generally short, typically less than two years, which offers investors faster liquidity.

Platform Issued Debt

Investors that invest in platform issued debt are investing in loans originated by the real estate crowdfunding site itself using investor funds. This means that investors' returns are usually 0.5 – 1% higher than with syndicated debt. Most of these loans are fix and flip loans and the annual fees are 0.5 -1.5%. The typical investment is for 6 months to two years.

Regardless of the specific type, the pros and cons of crowdfunding real estate loans include:

Pros:

A shorter timeline so you generally receive your money back within 6 months – 2 years.

Your money isn't tied up for a long period of time so you can invest in other projects.

Less risk than investing in equity because if the developer defaults, the investors can recoup their loss through a foreclosure.

Predictable payments usually paid monthly or quarterly, and the amounts are usually forecasted ahead of time.

Cons:

Typically higher fees for using the crowdfunding platform.

Lower return on investment than investing in equity; investments are generally capped by the interest rate on the loan.

DIFFERENCES BETWEEN EQUITY AND LENDING CROWDFUNDING

The phenomenon of real estate crowdfunding is currently a hot topic of the blogosphere and of general communication; as in many other cases, the fact of being a sector in its early days coincides with a misrepresentation of primary differences.

Many publications, from the most read to the most specialized of the sector, are helping to feed a heavy cloud of smoke around real estate crowdfunding. The most significant confusion, at the moment, is concentrated around the different types of business models and operativity of the platforms currently present on the Italian market; typically, lending crowdfunding and equity crowdfunding. We therefore, consider it particularly useful for the reader to try to identify, in the clearest possible manner, the structural differences within the national real estate crowdfunding landscape.

Premise: With Equal Risk, Equal Return

In the ideal financial strategy, the assumption of risk is rewarded by higher returns. Equally, in such a strategy, the average investor will try to maximize his income by hunting for opportunities by which, taking advantage of information or other benefits, he/she is able to extract a higher return than the actual risk of the transaction. The game is played by acknowledging a perceived risk as a non-existing risk, and therefore worthy of being snubbed.

Structural Asymmetry: Lending Vs. Equity

A first noticeable difference between crowdlending platforms in general, is the prospect of generally lower returns than equity platforms. We now want to investigate whether this disparity is attributable, or not, solely to the variable risk.

Lending crowdfunding distributes the funds collected by individuals or companies to the various creditors, spreading the risk together with the yield; equity crowdfunding, on the other hand, consists of a direct investment in a single entity, trying to capitalize the return from a single financial transaction. So far, nothing contradicts our premise.

However, there are risks that the investor may not have taken into account: to date, on the Italian market, any real estate crowdfunding operation that does not belong to the platforms authorized by the Consob, is not subject to control by Italian legislators. In the event of a dispute, therefore, expensive and unlikely legal actions can be expected outside the country, considering in particular the Insignificant the amounts involved. The transnational element is not a definitive condition of the Italian real estate market for crowdfunding, but it is good to take this into account.

Continuing our short investigation, we find another determining factor for the difference in returns: as we have already stressed elsewhere, equity crowdfunding opens up to the market of private investment, or that tier of investments that gets rid of intermediation layers, and with good reason!

In our view, the elimination of intermediation can be an added value only for some investors, certainly not for everyone, nor for the totality of their portfolio. Getting rid of the middleman can be attractive for those who have relevant information to invest in a given project, and real estate is one of the areas in which the information asymmetries are among the most determining factors for choosing a project. Showing the middleman the door, in these cases, has the advantage of sparing us from a series of commissions; as already well-documented by the Idealista, the business model of real estate lending crowdfunding platforms currently operating in Italy, ensures that the company withdraws 10% of the generated dividends.

One of the investment strategies that best fit with equity crowdfunding is the classic core-satellite, named by Nassim Taleb also as barbell strategy (balance sheet strategy): the portfolio consists of 80-85% of particularly liquid assets, and the remainder holds much more profitable assets. We'll talk about it soon in a future article.

Let us now turn to the question raw, unbridled risk. When we think about the alternative lending vs. equity, traditional financial instruments are divided into bonds and equity investments. A bond offers a generally lower return than shares: through a bond, the issuer promises the creditor to pay a price determined at maturity. The security of performance is traded based on its size. The problem with crowdlending operations lies in the fact that no bond is issued against the sums paid in the form of financing. We therefore have a similar risk between equity and lending in terms of guarantees, with very different returns. The investor of the equity platform, moreover, is a member regularly registered in the Chamber of Commerce, owner in all respects of a company, of equity and tangible assets; nothing comparable is offered by crowdlending.

The typically Italian image of real estate crowdfunding is crystallizing around the lending model; in our opinion, this misrepresentation does not do justice to the whole national panorama, but above all it risks depriving the investor of a much more promising instrument - the phenomenon of equity crowdfunding, a reality regulated by legislators. We hope that the results of the platforms, which will only emerge with time, will speak for themselves, corroborating what has been explained thus far.

Now be wise, and dig deeper. Dig deeper, uncover glory

BENEFITS & RISKS OF REAL ESTATE CROWDFUNDING

Real estate crowdfunding can provide an opportunity for investors to diversify their investments and reduce their risk while earning good returns on their investment. It allows investors to be a part of deals that were previously unattainable to them. However, it does have its own set of risks, such as if your project goes under and you lose your investment.

Benefits Of Investing In Real Estate:

It is simple to understand with no complex ratios or jargons to get your head around.

You can increase the value of the asset purchased by working on it (upgrading it). Other investment options like stocks or bonds don't offer this benefit.

Real Estate Investment offers a natural protection against inflation since property prices and rent increase with inflation rates.

You have a chance of finding a good deal if you research and analyze the market well.

The rental income offers a good second source of income and the property increases in value as time goes by.

Hence, you get regular passive income till you are leasing out the property and capital appreciation on sale.

Even if you have to take a housing loan to purchase the property, the rental income can help you to cover the instalments. So, your loan gets repaid while your property appreciates in value.

Real estate properties make good collateral for emergency loans.

Disadvantages Of Investing In Real Estate:

One of the biggest disadvantages of buying a property is the lack of liquidity. Unlike other assets, real estate cannot be sold quickly without drastically reducing the price.

Real Estate requires regular maintenance and care. This implies recurring costs and investment of time.

A housing loan can turn into a liability if you lose your primary source of income.

How Real Estate Crowdfunding Helps To Fight The Disadvantages:

Due to the potential of offering great returns, one cannot avoid investing in real estate. However, the disadvantages, as listed above, can work as a deterrent to many investors. Real Estate Crowdfunding takes the benefits of investing in real estate and eliminates the disadvantages of buying a property by offering a great alternative to invest in the realty market. Here is how Real Estate Crowdfunding works:

The Real Estate Crowdsourcing platform registers Investors and Borrowers by verifying their credentials.

Borrowers submit a project for which they need funding to the platform.

It verifies the details, runs some background checks and makes the project available to investors.

Investors assess the projects available based on their requirement and choose to invest completely or part of the amount requested.

Once the borrower manages to raise the entire amount, funds are disbursed.

It is well known that purchasing a property involves a huge amount of investment which is a disadvantage. Also, the regular maintenance and care require time and money. Crowdfunding takes both these aspects out of the equation. Many platforms allow investors to invest as low as $5,000 and participate in the real estate market. This ensures that you don't need to take a housing loan to add real estate as an asset class to your portfolio. Further, it offers equity investment through crowdsourcing making your investments liquid. You also don't need to worry about the maintenance of the property since the platform takes care of it too.

In a nutshell, Real Estate Crowdfunding helps in eliminating the disadvantages of real estate investments by spreading the investment amount across multiple borrowers. Having said that, there are certain risks associated with Real Estate Crowdfunding too.

Risks:

Most real estate investors are not market experts who can analyze and assess real estate projects easily. So, when you decide to invest through a real estate Crowdfunding platform, how do you assess any project? Most investors rely on the platform to provide good deals which do not require assessment or analysis. This can be counterproductive and pose a risk to investors.

Another risk is that of the Crowdfunding platform going under. Many platforms are now hiring a third-party bank as a custodian of their assets. This can work as a hedge against this risk.

Being new in the market, real estate Crowdfunding landscape needs understanding before you sign the dotted line. Equity / Debt investments, private or publicly traded, public but not listed investments; ensure that you understand these aspects well.

Diversification is known as the key to managing risks in almost all investment vehicles. Real Estate Crowdfunding is no different. While REITs offer an inherent diversification in a portfolio, with Crowdfunding, you need to ensure that you create a diversified portfolio to have a lower loan-to-value ratio.

Finally, the government has started putting some regulations in place for the Crowdfunding market. While the regulations are usually in favor of the investors, there might be some changes which can lead to an increase in charges or slow down the process.

WHO REAL ESTATE CROWDFUNDING IS RIGHT FOR

Real estate crowdfunding is right for passive investors who want access to real estate investments that they couldn't afford or wouldn't have access to on their own. It can also be right for investors who want to increase their exposure to debt.

Real estate crowdfunding is right for the following:

Investors who don't have enough capital to purchase a property outright but still want to invest in the real estate market.

Individuals looking for an alternative to investing in a REIT or in the stock market since it gives them access to properties otherwise unattainable.

Investors who don't want the headaches of being a landlord and who don't want to do any work themselves.

Individuals who want to invest in real estate outside of their own location, but otherwise wouldn't have the means or logistics to do so.

Real estate crowdfunding isn't right for you if you want to own the asset outright. It's also not right for you if you want to be a hands on investor and choose finishes and be in charge of deadlines, budgeting, and managing contractors. Investing in real estate crowdfunding is a much more passive investment.

If real estate crowdfunding isn't for you because you're interested in investing in real estate and want to be actively involved, consider purchasing a foreclosed property and fix it up and rent it. Check out our article on how to become a landlord for more information.

Accredited vs Non Accredited Real Estate Investors

Real estate crowdfunding sites cater to either accredited or non accredited investors. This will determine which sites you qualify to invest in. The Securities & Exchange Commission (SEC) determines the eligibility qualifications of accredited investors.

You're considered an accredited investor if you meet one of the following three criteria:

Individual income of $200,000+ or joint income of $300,000+ for the past 2 years

Individual or joint net worth of $1 million+, excluding the value of a primary residence

General partner, director, or executive officer for the issuer of non regulated securities

You're considered a non accredited investor if you don't meet the financial qualifications of an accredited investor mentioned above. It's important to know the difference between accredited and non accredited investors because some real estate crowdfunding sites allow both types of investors to invest, while others allow only accredited investors to invest.

SECRETS TO CROWDFUNDING REAL ESTATE

A real estate professional shares his experience and tips as a real estate crowdfunding investor

Real estate crowdfunding is quickly becoming the new alternative asset class of choice for investors. I've shared my experience investing on RealtyShares and PeerStreet here on the blog but wanted to get another investor's perspective on a different website.

The VP of Communications, Soren Godbersen, at EquityMultiple reached out after he read a few of my real estate investing articles. I was immediately interested in the company's institutional-level investments and as the only online investment platform backed by an established real estate firm.

For another perspective, I reached out to another long-time real estate crowdfunding investor.

Steve is a Portfolio Manager at a Los Angeles-based investment firm for commercial real estate investors. He agreed to an interview about his experience with real estate crowdfunding and the EquityMultiple platform.

The interview revealed a lot of great information on how to invest in crowdfunding real estate, so much so that I considered making this a series instead of just one long article.

You might not be able to finish the whole article at once so bookmark it and come back if you need to because there are some gold nuggets here to really get you started right in real estate crowdfunding.

What got you interested in real estate crowdfunding?

Steve: I have been in the commercial real estate business for over 20 years and have always had an affinity for the space. My firm is an institutional investment advisor and as a public company we are closely regulated on what types of individual investments we can make.

The real estate crowdfunding platform is allowed and thus gives me access to the private investment market. I like that you can review and essentially underwrite each deal to see how it fits into your portfolio.

Joseph: What really struck me interviewing Steve is the fact that he works in traditional commercial real estate investment and has chosen to get into crowdfunding as well. Here's a guy with all the access to traditional real estate investment you could hope for and he's active in real estate crowdfunding.

If that's not a vote of confidence for investing in crowdfunded real estate, I don't know what is.

My own real estate background started in college with a part-time position as a commercial real estate analyst for

CB Richard Ellis. Real estate is like no other investment and I love the combination of developing a physical asset and solid cash flows.

I've been investing directly in properties since my mid-20s but have always run up against the biggest hurdle in real estate investing, diversification. It's all but impossible for individual investors to diversify a portfolio of properties with less than a million. That means buying different property types in different regions.

Buy less than a dozen or more properties across the U.S. and you expose yourself to regional crashes and weakness in a particular type of property.

That's where real estate crowdfunding comes in. For just a few thousand on each deal, you can diversify your traditional investment portfolio with properties all over the country. Even better, each property is professionally-managed so the investment doesn't add to your workload.

Have you invested in traditional real estate or REITs?

Steve: Yes, I have been involved in direct ownership of real estate and have owned a number of publicly traded REITs over the years.

Joseph: I think a lot of investors look at the different types of real estate investing as an either-or situation. They figure they own a few shares of real estate investment trusts (REITs) so why would they need to own property directly or through real estate crowdfunding.

real estate crowdfunding investor interviews for investorsEach method of real estate investing carries its own advantages and limitations, making the best portfolio one that incorporates them all.

Direct Property Investment: Offers the highest return if you can develop and manage your own property but can be a huge burden for individual investors. Direct ownership also offers a great tax deduction against other income.

The problem with buying property directly is a double-whammy. It can cost millions to buy enough individual properties to diversify away your risks. Even if you're able to do that, managing all those properties yourself is a full-time job.

REIT Investment: REITs are special companies that own and manage commercial real estate, usually in a specific property type. They trade just like stocks so are easy to buy and you get professional management. The companies avoid corporate income taxes if they pay out most of their income to investors, meaning these real estate investments provide consistent cash flow.

The problem with REITs is the cost structure. You pay for that professional management through operating costs of the company plus you pay an annual fee on the shares. REITs are also exposed to stock market risks so they don't offer exactly the same protections as the other two ways to invest in real estate.

Real Estate Crowdfunding Investment: Is like a hybrid model between the other two ways to invest in real estate investing. You get direct ownership in properties and that diversification but also the property management by a professional developer.

There are two problems with real estate crowdfunding, as I see it. While the crowdfunding platforms do their own analysis to check developers and properties, you still need to do some of your own analysis. Starting a real estate investing group to share in the analysis work is a great idea for new investors.

Also, most of the deals tend to be on short-term projects of five years or less. That means you'll need to look for investments more often than you would a longer-term investment in a property or a REIT.

Any real estate investment is going to offer protection against runaway inflation, solid long-term returns and diversification of your risks from a stock/bond portfolio. The amount of your wealth you hold in real estate might vary by age and your own investing needs but everyone should have some property in their portfolio.

No other investment has created as much family wealth as real estate. That should tell you something.

In how many real estate crowdfunding deals have you participated?

Steve: I have participated in 14 deals over the past two years.

Joseph: One of the benefits to real estate crowdfunding is the ability to get access to deals all across the country and in different property types for a fraction of the cost compared to traditional property investing. That means building your portfolio to ten or more deals.

The different property types include:

- Office
- Warehouse
- Hotel & Leisure
- Self-Storage
- Retail
- Industrial
- Residential

Just as with investing in stocks of companies in different sectors, investing in different property types will help protect you against economic events. Some property types are exposed to rising interest rates while others are relatively immune. Some property types follow the business cycle, as with office rents, while others have more constant demand.

Since most real estate crowdfunding sites only get a few new deals a month, it's easier to build a solid portfolio if you're investing on more than one site. That's why I invest on multiple platforms, to get access to the best deals and build a portfolio faster.

How much do you invest in each crowdfunding deal, on average?

Steve: One of the attractive things of crowdfunding vehicles is the relatively small investment increments that are allowed. I typically invest $20,000-40,000 in each deal but that will obviously vary for each investor.

I try to weigh how much of my portfolio to carry in illiquid investments, and then try to balance my real estate portfolio by various risk factors (property type, location, sponsor, etc.)

Joseph: The minimum investment per property will vary from platform to platform. I've found that deals on RealtyShares generally require an investment from $1,000 to $5,000 while those on PeerStreet is $1,000 per loan. The larger, institutional-level deals on EquityMultiple usually means minimums are higher, between $5,000 and $10,000 per deal.

That's still a fraction of what it would cost you to develop your own real estate project. With real estate crowdfunding, an individual investor can easily put together a diversified portfolio for less than $20,000 in equity and debt investments.

What are three things you look for in the best real estate crowdfunding deals?

Steve: I would say the three primary things that I review very closely in each deal are the property, market conditions and business plan feasibility of the sponsor.

I want to make sure that the sponsor's business plan makes sense given the property and market they are targeting, so I look carefully at the underlying projections to see if they make sense versus other alternatives in the marketplace. In all these factors, I look at the scenarios that are provided by EquityMultiple, and usually overlay my own set of projections to see what the range of outcomes looks like.

Joseph: I could write a book on real estate analysis so it's tough to pinpoint just a few things real estate crowdfunding investors should look for in a deal. It's one of the limitations of the investment, the work that needs to go in to analyzing your potential deals.

All the crowdfunding platforms have their own staff that investigate the developer (sponsor), the property and the numbers behind the deal. RealtyShares reports that just 5% of the deals submitted to its site end up making it in front of investors. That said, you still need to do a little homework yourself to make sure an investment looks good and fits with your portfolio.

Real Estate Crowdfunding Investment Process: Ask yourself these questions for every deal

How much experience does the developer have and have they managed this kind of a project before?

Do I need this type of property or regional exposure in my portfolio or am I already diversified in the area?

Who else is financing the project and what are their rights to the property?

Are there any zoning issues that still need resolved or does the developer have a greenlight?

How does the potential return for the project stack up against other similar projects?

Is the timeline for the project realistic compared to other deals?

What are the biggest assumptions on which the developer is relying to meet projections? Compare these assumptions like property value, rent increases, vacancy rates against averages in the local market.

Analyzing your own real estate crowdfunding deals can be a little overwhelming at first but can also be a lot of fun. The platforms do a good job of vetting deals and laying out the risks so that's useful when you're first starting. It also helps to diversify across as many deals as possible so one property won't break your portfolio if the return turns out to be less than expected.

Are there any warning signs new real estate crowdfunding investors should watch for in a bad deal?

Steve: It is really hard to define a "bad" deal per se, as much of the investment decision comes down to the individual investor's risk tolerance and goals for an investment. That said, I think there are certainly some red flags that can emerge that new crowdfunding investors should be wary of.

Look carefully at the business plan and see if the projected cash flow and exit strategies make sense. Are there comparable lease and property sales to support the assumptions? I am always wary of deals that are fully dependent upon a future sale as the driver of returns, unless the returns are very high and the assumptions are sound.

Another red flag is if a sponsor has very little experience or is branching out into a market or property type that they don't have a stable track record.

Joseph: Steve's point about deal returns contingent on a future sale is an important one. I also like to see that the property can yield a solid return on the basis of rents rather than on a high sales price.

Most real estate crowdfunding deals are short-term developments or flips. The project return will usually be dependent on the sales price but that doesn't mean there is no potential return from rents. I like to see deals where the developer has the option to provide a good rent return if sales prices fall apart and they have to hold onto the property for a while longer.

Have you recorded any returns yet on any crowdfunding deals?

Steve: I have had one deal that was a 9-month bridge loan that fully paid off as expected with a 9%+ annualized yield. My portfolio is a mixture of mostly equity holdings that are a combination of solid current returns or are development plays that have a higher expected return once completed. About 75% of my portfolio is providing solid ongoing cash returns, and the remaining 25% is slated for a more speculative IRR.

Joseph: The real estate crowdfunding sites are hesitant to talk about returns for regulatory concerns, not wanting to seem like they are being promotional. With real estate crowdfunding being as new as it is, it's tough to forecast returns over the long-run.

Real estate crowdfunding returns should be at least comparable to the return on equity REITs, maybe even higher. That would mean annual returns to property investors of around 15% over the long-term. Even accounting for the biggest real estate bust in U.S. history, equity investment in real estate still easily beat the return on stocks in the 20 years through 2016.

Large equity REIT companies don't have the flexibility or speed that smaller crowdfunding developers have so I wouldn't be surprised if real estate crowdfunding investors see returns a percent or two higher than REITs on an annualized basis.

Real estate crowdfunding returns will vary by type of investment as well. PeerStreet, which specializes in debt investments, quotes historical returns between 6% and 12% annually. Double-digit returns on safe debt investments is unheard of in traditional bond investing unless you're buying the bonds of bankrupt countries like Venezuela.

Returns on equity crowdfunding will be higher but with more risk. Deals generally quote projected returns from 9% to 15% on most platforms which means you're probably looking at a blended return of 10% to 12% after accounting for deals that don't meet expectations.

Even a return of 9% annually on real estate crowdfunding would be excellent considering you're also getting a diversifier from other assets in your portfolio. This is a point too often neglected when investors look at the different asset classes. Even traditional bonds with meager annual returns of 5% are a critical addition for their ability to reduce your risk from the roller-coaster stock market.

How do you judge whether the developer has the necessary skills to be successful?

Steve: As noted above, I generally take a look at their history. Even if they are relatively new to the real estate development arena, most of the sponsors that I have reviewed have a fairly strong real estate investment background. I often look at the websites, reviews of currently owned properties or even call people I know in the industry to see if they have good references.

Joseph: The platforms do a good job at vetting deal sponsors but it's always good to do your own homework as well. There are enough crowdfunding deals available that you don't need to invest with a questionable developer just to put your money to work.

In real estate crowdfunding, as with any investment, it's better to let a few diamonds go by than to invest in every opportunity and get stuck with a lump of coal.

I start by checking the public profiles of the development team, especially LinkedIn, to make sure they match with what is said on the crowdfunding platform. You'd be amazed at what you can find with a simple Google search. You can also check with the county assessor to make sure the property is registered to the sponsor or development team.

How do you estimate the potential return on real estate crowdfunding deals?

Steve: EquityMultiple does a very good job of providing projected returns and the background cash flows that are used in the assumptions. I look at the projections and then try to overlay my own assumptions on them. EM also provides a range of outcomes including optimistic and pessimistic that gives an investor a feel for the range of likely outcomes.

I can't say that I have a specific cut-off return for a go/no-go decision. That return threshold will depend on the underlying risk of the transaction. I generally try to build my portfolio with a mixture of stable properties that have durable current income streams and then blend in some higher-risk transactions that can provide a much higher return.

Each investor has to determine what other alternative investments are available and then assess how each real estate investment fits into their objectives.

Joseph: All the real estate crowdfunding sites have analysts that check projections on projects to give investors an idea of projected returns. Doing some additional analysis and with a little experience, you'll quickly get an idea of how to adjust projected returns higher or lower on your own assumptions.

Just as you need to diversify your overall wealth in different assets by investing in stocks, bonds and real estate, you should also diversify within each asset. You do this in your real estate portfolio by investing across property types, regions and types of deals. Steve shares a great idea here to build a base of investments with solid income and then add some higher-risk, higher-return deals as they come along.

What else should new real estate crowdfunding investors know to be successful?

Steve: I would say that to be successful in real estate crowdfunding, and investor should have some defined objectives that they are trying to meet in this space. Real estate can provide a number of attractive opportunities such as diversification, current income and possible inflation hedging, but not all deals are created equal.

Investors should be prepared to "dig in" to each deal and understand that this is an illiquid investment that you just can't sell out of on a whim. Given that your eventual performance is many factors are outside of your control, you should enter each deal with your eyes wide open. I really enjoy diving into the analysis and studying the business plan closely. Though it can be challenging, it is often quite rewarding and a lot of fun!

Joseph: Steve makes another great point about real estate crowdfunding being an 'illiquid' investment. That means you can't just sell your investment like you can in stocks. Judging from investors' tendency to panic-selling in the stock market, it might actually be a good thing that you're locked into the investment for a few years.

Most real estate crowdfunding deals are termed from one to five years so it's not like you are locked into the property for decades anyway.

There were a lot of great ideas for real estate crowdfunding investors and I want to highlight a few as a summary.

Real estate crowdfunding is a great way to diversify your other real estate investments in property and REITs.

Invest in multiple deals on multiple platforms to get access to as many opportunities as possible and reduce your risk around any one deal.

Do your homework on each deal, checking projections for the property, market conditions and on the developer.

Look for properties that can provide a solid real estate income return besides the potential on a quick sale at a higher price.

Real estate crowdfunding returns of 10% and higher are just part of the story along with a chance to diversify your risks in stocks and bonds.

Understand that real estate crowdfunding is an illiquid investment and you'll have to hold properties for the duration of the project.

TOP BEST REAL ESTATE CROWDFUNDING SITE

Fundrise

Established in 2010, Fundrise is one of the pioneers in the online real estate crowdfunding space. This platform gives users and investors the chance to benefit from real estate offerings for only a few hundred dollars ($500 for an initial investment).

Fundrise also introduced electronic Real Estate Investment Trust (eREIT) last 2015 to make investing in commercial real estate available to the majority of investors. It's like you're investing to an ETF or mutual fund.

As you sign up in the platform, you'll invest either in one of the three Core Portfolio plans or in the low-minimum Starter Portfolio. Whatever you choose, your money will be invested in an allocated assortment of eFunds and eREITs consisting of private real estate assets located across the United States. You can receive your payouts in 2 different ways — either by (1) quarterly dividend distributions or (2) appreciation in asset value at the end of your asset's investment term.

Realty Mogul

Realty Mogul is an online real estate capital marketplace platform founded by Jilliene Helman and Justin Hughes. Began in 2013, To change and disrupt the traditional real estate funding by building an online crowdfunding website is their aim in creating this platform.

The Realty Mogul platform claims more than 130,000 sponsors, borrowers, and investors as per writing, and is staffed by a group of experts who have a mix of experience in finance, real estate, and technology. It has given financing for more than 350 real estate properties, with advances totaling more than $280 million.

Realty Mogul introduced a MogulREIT to compete with Fundrise's eREITs. The advantages of a MogulREIT is (1) no accreditation is required, (2) more broadening at a lower sum required than putting resources into individual properties, and (3) normally lower investment prerequisite than a private placement.

CrowdStreet

CrowdStreet has one of the largest and most diverse selections in the business and specializes in commercial real estate (CRE) investments. One of the good points in partnering CrowdStreet is that it enables the speculator to collaborate specifically with the mediator, as opposed to placing itself in the middle of all communication.

Crowdstreet sources deals from mediators, and then makes those available on its website. Just note that the client still needs to pay expenses and remuneration charged by the outside support, which change from deal to deal.

Patch Of Land

Patch of Land is a Peer-to-Real-Estate lending marketplace that matches accredited and institutional investors seeking high-yield, short-term, asset-collateralized investments to borrowers seeking more timely and consistent sources of funding for rehabbing properties across America.

Their goal is to solve the problem of inefficient, fragmented, and opaque real estate private lending by using technology and data-driven processes to create transparency and to efficiently underwrite projects for borrowers with real estate projects that are routinely bypassed by traditional lenders.

As per InvestorJunkie review about PoL, Patch of Land's lending platform achieves their mission to reduce the cost and increase the efficiency of getting these deals approved and funded. If you're looking to invest in short-term debt with generous yields, then PoL may be right for you.

RealtyShares

RealtyShares is a real estate investment platform that gives investors direct access to quality investment opportunities and real estate operators the ability to raise capital. From the partnerships they develop with real estate sponsors to the service they deliver to their investors, their mission is to connect the capital to opportunity. They see potential in delivering value and efficiency to real estate investors and operators through their expertise, technology, and data.

RealCrowd

Real Crowd, just like CrowdStreet, is focusing on Commercial Real Estate (CRE) assets. It offers both equity and debt deals, as well as both single property investments and multi-property assets. Because they make their money by charging the sponsor, they don't charge clients an extra fee. They're also one of the few sites in this business that increased their volume since last year.

Fund That Flip

Fund That Flip works in residential debt investments (also called hard money loans or fix-and-flip loans), alongside a little background of multifamily and business debt. They have the lowest LTV (loan to values) of any platform (higher values have more risk than the lower).

Fund That Flip credits cash to borrowers and afterward sells pieces of those loans to investors who share in the profit (or loss). Typically the borrower is purchasing the house and renovating it with the purpose of selling it at a higher price. Lastly, Fund That Flip has great straightforwardness and a best-of-breed low default rate.

Walliance

Walliance is the first Italian equity crowdfunding platform for the real estate market. We guarantee Italian savers real estate investment opportunities starting from € 500, and we offer to the operators of the sector the possibility to raise capital in an alternative and transparent way.

Our project was created from a simple, but revolutionary concept: taming the technological and financial innovations that the global economy is going through (first of all crowdfunding), and thus breaking down the barriers to entry in an investment sector traditionally prohibitive for the small-medium saver.

We have been operating in the Italian market since September 2017, but our history is deeply rooted. Bertoldi Group, a family-owned company from which Walliance took its first steps, has positioned itself for years in the real estate sector, developing property management, consulting, and real estate investments. To these, were added numerous holdings in the Fintech, sector, among which the world leader for equity crowdfunding Crowdcube stands out.

We have closely observed the unfolding of Italian crowdfunding from its origins, assessing its potential for development. At the same time, we were aware of the historical performance of the Real Estate sector, despite the decline of 2008: what better scope for crowdfunding than an investment sector that has historically proved to be among the best performing? The long path to tune that initial intuition to the strict Italian regulations thus began, rewarded by the CONSOB with the authorization to operate on the national market as the first equity crowdfunding Real Estate platform.

Currently, Forbes estimates the global market Real Estate equity crowdfunding market has reached over 4.3 billion dollars, and is poised to reach 300 billion by 2025. We have positioned ourselves on the Italian territory, collecting 1.6 million euros in four months, between registrations and pre-registrations, with real estate projects on Trento, Milan and New York. At the end of

2017, Walliance completed a round of investments of €
750k, and looks with optimism to the European
Commission's maneuvers for the creation of a unified
investment-based crowdfunding market: the international
ascent has just begun.

Housers

Housers is a real estate crowdfunding site founded in 2016
in Spain and has close to 100,000 users making it the
biggest platform on the list based on users. To me, it
seems like one of the most professionally driven platforms
out there.

Housers is a great platform with many opportunities to
invest in real estate through buy-to-let, buy-to-sell and
development loans. There's actually also a possibility to
invest in art loans. The platform has a great overview of
your investments and very detailed loan information. The
properties listed for investment are complete with
pictures and floor plans. I also like that Housers has a
secondary marketplace if you wan to cash out early.
Compared to other platforms, you cannot sell your
loans/projects on a premium or a discount, which is both
good and bad. Housers' customer service explained it like
this:

"You can't choose the price of the shares because of laws of our regulator. The Marketplace is only a liquidity window for the investors so they can sell the shares at the same price and exit a project or invest in one."

CONCLUSION

Real estate crowdfunding allows investors to diversify their investment portfolio by investing in projects that they otherwise wouldn't be able to afford. It also gives borrowers access to more capital in a shorter time frame. Although rewards can be lucrative, it's a fairly new concept and there are risks involved, so it's important to do your research.

In truth, real estate crowdfunding has proved popular and works well when it comes to mobilising funds for real estate projects.

Unlike banks and other brokers, crowdfunding platforms make the whole deal easy and fast thanks to innovative tech solutions and simplified procedures.

Both investors and borrowers tend to find it as a godsend.

Limited Liability - Disclaimer

Please note that the content of this book is based on personal experience and various information sources, and it is only for personal use.

Please note the information contained within this document is for educational and entertainment purposes only and no warranties of any kind are declared or implied.

Readers acknowledge that the author is not engaging in the rendering of legal, financial or professional advice. Please consult a licensed professional before attempting any techniques outlined in this book.

Nothing in this book is intended to replace common sense or legal accounting, or professional advice and is meant only to inform.

Your particular circumstances may not be suited to the example illustrated in this book; in fact, they likely will not be.

You should use the information in this book at your own risk. The reader is responsible for his or her actions.

The information provided herein is stated to be truthful and consistent, in that any liability, in terms of inattention or otherwise, by any usage or abuse of any policies, processes, or directions contained within is the solitary and utter responsibility of the recipient reader.

By reading this book, the reader agrees that under no circumstances is the author responsible for any losses, direct or indirect, which are incurred as a result of the use of the information contained within this document, including, but not limited to, errors, omissions, or inaccuracies.

Do not go yet; One last thing to do

If you enjoyed this book or found it useful I'd be very grateful if you'd post a short review on Amazon. Your support really does make a difference and I read all the reviews personally so I can get your feedback and make this book even better.

Thanks again for your support!

Printed by Amazon Italia Logistica S.r.l.
Torrazza Piemonte (TO), Italy

57557394R10039